# HOW TO LIVE LIKE

# A CARIBBEAN
# PIRATE

Thanks to the creative team:
Senior Editor: Alice Peebles
Consultant: John Haywood
Fact checking: Kate Mitchell
Design: www.collaborate.agency

Hungry Tomato™
A division of Lerner Publishing Group, Inc.
241 First Avenue North
Minneapolis, MN 55401 USA

For reading levels and more information,
look up this title at www.lernerbooks.com.

Main body text set in Century Gothic Regular 10/13.
Typeface provided by Monotype Typography.

**Library of Congress Cataloging-in-Publication Data**

Names: Farndon, John, author. | Campidelli, Maurizio, 1962–
illustrator.
Title: How to live like a Caribbean pirate / author, John Farndon ;
illustrator, Maurizio Campidelli.
Description: Minneapolis : Hungry Tomato, 2017. | Includes index. |
Audience: Ages 8-12.
Identifiers: LCCN 2015046901 (print) | LCCN 2016004622 (ebook) |
ISBN 9781512406313 (lb : alk. paper) | ISBN 9781512411621
(pb : alk. paper) | ISBN 9781512409185 (eb pdf)
Subjects:  LCSH: Pirates—Juvenile literature.
Classification: LCC G535 .F28 2017 (print) | LCC G535 (ebook) |
DDC 910.4/5—dc23

LC record available at http://lccn.loc.gov/2015046901

Manufactured in the United States of America
1 – VP – 7/15/16

# HOW TO LIVE LIKE
# A CARIBBEAN
# PIRATE

By John Farndon
Illustrated by Tatio Viano

HUNGRY
TOMATO.

# contents

# Pirate!

It's the year 1717, and you're in the city of Charleston in the North Carolina colony. My name is Jamie Flynn. There's a forest of ships tied up against the pier. Some ships have slaves from Africa. Others are headed back to Europe.

But who are those shifty-looking men over there? *Uh-oh*! They've spotted me listening. They're coming this way! *Agh*, too late! Before I can struggle, they've put a sack over my head, and thrown me into a rowboat. "Sharp eyes, eh? He's just what we need for a lookout!" Then it all goes black. I've been kidnapped by pirates!

## Golden Age of Piracy

Between 1716 and 1726, pirate ships roamed the seas near America and into the Caribbean. Many a lone ship caught sight of a pirate ship racing toward them over the waves and knew they were doomed. Historians now call it the Golden Age of Piracy. But for the victims of pirates it was anything but golden! Pirate leaders such as Black Bart, Black Sam Bellamy, and Calico Jack were ruthless cutthroats, and you didn't want to be on a ship attacked by one of them!

Florida

Gulf of Mexico

Cuba

Dominican Republic

Caribbean Sea

If you live in a seaport, you'd better watch out for "press gangs"—ruthless gangs that recruit pirates by force!

# A Pirate Ship

Oh no! It seems I've been taken aboard the most fearsome of all pirate ships, the *Queen Anne's Revenge*, flagship of the terrifying pirate Blackbeard.

Like nearly all pirate ships, *Queen Anne's Revenge* is a stolen ship. To make it fast and dangerous, the pirates stripped away its cumbersome "castles," the deck structures at front and back. Then they knocked through the lower decks to open it up so it could take lots of extra men. And they cut holes in the hull to poke forty cannons through. That makes it a formidable ship for fast attack! Unarmed ships better watch out!

## Blackbeard's Ship

In 1996, divers found a wreck lying in 28 feet (8.5 meters) of water just off Atlantic Beach in North Carolina. In 2011, the National Geographic Society confirmed that this was *Queen Anne's Revenge*, run aground in 1718, complete with a cannon. Among the thousands of items found was a medical syringe showing that Blackbeard did look after his crew!

North Carolina

Atlantic Ocean

A cutaway of the
*Queen Anne's Revenge*

## Beached!

It's hard to keep a pirate ship in tip-top condition, because we can't go into any regular port for maintenance. We have to steal all the equipment we need from the ships we attack. And every now and then, we need to run the ship aground to scrape the hull clean of barnacles and weeds that might slow us down. That's seriously hard work!

# Life on Board

"UP THE MAST, BOY! NOW!" That's the mate yelling! Because I'm small and light, and have sharp eyes, I'm the lookout in the crow's nest—the most dangerous part of the ship! It's the tiny bucket right up at the top of the main mast, swaying more than 50 feet (15 m) above the deck.

I often have to climb up slippery, wet rigging as gales are howling and waves crash over the ship. It's really, really frightening when the ship rolls over, the mast leans and I'm left hanging high out over the crashing waves. I feel sick most of the time! The last lookout before me crashed to his death on the deck when his foot got caught by a stray sail line. But I can see a long way from up here—and if I'm the first to see a ship for us to attack, I'll get a reward of one gold piece!

Some of our crew were kidnapped like me, but many chose to come. Life is tough on other ships and on land, too, now. Being a pirate is dangerous, but you've got the freedom of the sea.

## Below Decks

Life on a pirate ship is no fun at all! The food's just stale biscuits and, if I'm lucky, a bit of salt beef so tough it'd be easier to eat my shoes (if I had any!). And there are no beds—just hammocks for the senior crew. Lookout boys like me just curl up on ropes or sacking below deck. It's really cold and wet and dark, and the smell is terrible. *Ugh!* AND there are RATS!

# Blackbeard!

Oh no! I'm being hauled up before the captain, the monstrous Blackbeard. His real name is Edward Teach, and he probably came from a decent British family. But he's called Blackbeard because of his huge black beard. It's no ordinary beard, I can tell you! It's huge and dark and knotted into plaits that look like writhing snakes. And when he goes into battle, he often ties lighted fireworks into them to make himself look super scary! And now he's shouting at me like an angry bear!

They say Blackbeard is so strong he can cut a man in half with a single blow from his cutlass. And he's so nasty, he shot his own mate in the knees just for a laugh! But maybe he spreads these rumors himself. If his victims believe he's so dreadful, they'll give up without a fight when they hear Blackbeard is coming. . . I'm sure he just winked at me!

## Kinds of Pirates

The "buccaneers" of the 1600s were pirates given "letters of marque" by the French and British so they could legally raid Spanish enemy ships. A "buccan" was the beach barbeque they liked. "Privateers" were private ships hired by governments to attack enemies. "Corsairs" were what the English called French pirates, and what the French called Muslim pirates. "Barbary pirates" were Muslim pirates from the Barbary Coast of North Africa.

## Here are some other scary pirates:

**Captain Kidd:** Hanged 1701, London. Best prize: the *Quedagh Merchant*'s silks and gold

**Black Bart Roberts:** Killed 1722, off Nigeria in Africa. Best prize: fifteen ships in three days!

**Henry Morgan:** Died 1688, Jamaica. Best prize: Destroying the Spanish fleet in Venezuela

**Sam Bellamy:** Died 1717, in a storm. Best prize: *Whydah*'s indigo, gold, and silver

**Calico Jack Rackham:** Hanged 1720, Jamaica. Crew included two women captured with him (right)

**Anne Bonny and Mary Read:** Escaped hanging because they were pregnant. Read died 1721. Bonny's end is uncertain.

# Walking the Plank!

Pirates look after each other well in a tight situation. But they're really brutal if anyone crosses them—and I mean BRUTAL! It's amazing how many different ways they've found to punish those who rub a pirate crew the wrong way! These are just some of the ways that pirates make anyone regret upsetting them. . .

**WARNING!**

Never cross a pirate or else any of these bad things might happen to you...

**Marooning:** Deserters are left on a desert island with a gun and a bottle of rum. The rum is for courage to shoot himself—or he could just starve to death.

**Keelhauling:** This is a particularly nasty punishment. We tie the victim's hands and feet and haul him right under the bottom of the boat (the keel).

**Shooting:** We can just shoot wrongdoers, but the cruelest pirates prolong the agony by shooting them in the knee. Then, they'll be crippled for life.

**Walking the plank:** Everyone thinks pirates make their enemies walk off the end of a plank blindfolded into the sea. But this is just a myth.

**Dunking:** If we don't want to kill him, but just get him really worried, we'll string him up by his hands from the yard arm—the horizontal arm that holds the sails.

**Flogging:** The cat-o'-nine-tails is not a fluffy kitten—it's a particularly nasty whip made of nine ropes with knotted ends.

**Clapping in irons:** Of course, some victims are just locked in wrist and leg irons and thrown into the ship's hold.

## The Pirate Code

Pirates may be lawless, but we have our rules! When anyone joins the crew, they must sign the Articles of Agreement—or else. The Articles are a list of rules on how to behave, how to divide up the loot, and what compensation you get if you're badly injured.

## Typical Pirate Rules:

1. Every man has a vote in what to do.

2. Every man has a share in the booty.

3. No one is to play cards or dice for money.

4. Lights and candles must be out at 8 o'clock at night.

5. Pistols and cutlasses must be kept clean and fit for service.

6. No women are allowed on board.

7. Desertion in battle will be punished with death or marooning.

8. No one is to strike another on board. All quarrels must be ended on shore, at sword and pistol.

9. If any man should lose a limb, he is to get eight hundred dollars.

10. The captain and quartermaster are to receive two shares of a prize; the master, boatswain, and gunner, one share and a half; and other officers one share and a quarter.

# cutlass and Flintlock

Sometimes, ships surrender without a fight as soon as they see a pirate ship heading toward them. But if they don't, we may need to fight and overpower them. There are no passengers on a pirate ship—we all fight. So we all need weapons. Out at sea, we can't buy them from a store, can we? So we have to steal them from the ships we attack—or we improvise. Some of the things we use weren't made as weapons.

## WARNING!

If you see a small black ball that doesn't explode coming your way—you'd still better be careful. It might just be a stinkpot that sends out foul-smelling fumes.

## Armed like a pirate...
A pirate needs weapons that allow you to fight hand-to-hand in tight spaces between the rigging.

**Cutlass:** A pirate's favorite sword is short, but heavy enough to slash rope—or an arm.

**Belaying pin:** This is for securing ropes, but it's great for knocking your foe on the head!

**Grappling hook:** Chuck several over to your target ship, and yank it in close!

**Sword:** Some pirates choose a small sword for stabbing at the enemy, rather than a cutlass.

**Flintlock:** Blackbeard straps six to his waist ready to fire at the pull of a strip of silk.

**Grenades:** Light the fuse of these gunpowder-filled iron or clay balls, toss, and... boom!

**Boarding ax:** Grab one to hack away at rigging—and your foe.

**Marlin spike:** Undo knots in the rigging with this, and use it as a dagger.

**Caltrop or crowsfoot:** Throw several on deck for cutting into feet.

**Buckler:** It may look like a small shield, but it's for punching and slashing.

# Sneaky Tactics

"Ship ahoy!" I shout as I spy a treasure ship sailing away in the distance. Blackbeard is thrilled—we haven't seen a ship for weeks and things were getting desperate. The chase is on! But it's not easy capturing a ship at sea. First you've got to get close. If it was heading this way, we could run up a false distress flag so the ship comes to help. The famous pirate Anne Bonny once got her crew to cover themselves in red paint and pretend to be dead after a battle! This tactic won't work for us, though, because our potential victims are sailing away from us.

We've caught up! But we want our prize in one piece. So first we fire a warning shot across its bows and tell it to heave to (stop). That's scary enough for most ships, I can tell you. But this ship is not heaving to. Now we get serious! We pull alongside, so our cannons face it. Fire!!! We just want to slow it down, though. So we aim high above the hull and shoot away from the rigging. The sails flap loose, and the ship drifts to a standstill. . .

Pirates made sure their ships were kept as light as possible. That way they could catch up with merchant ships slowed down by their cargo. Many pirates sailed in sloops, which were the fastest ships on the sea. Some could sail at more than 11 knots (12.6 miles per hour).

# Death is coming...

Pirates have such a fearsome reputation that sometimes we only have to run up our pirate flag to scare a ship into surrender. The flag's black and marked with a skull and crossbones! Some call it Captain Death. Others call it the Jolly Roger—but there's nothing jolly about it!

# Stand by to Board!

Now we're pulling right alongside. Some men fling over grappling hooks and begin to yank the ships together. As we close in, men up in the rigging spray the deck with shot from blunderbuss rifles. The crew of the prize ship run for cover. Blackbeard yells, "Stand by to board!" Oh yes, we're ready, armed to the teeth with stinkpots and grenades, spikes and pins, and cutlasses and crowsfeet. Up above, men are already swinging across, cutlasses and axes in hand, to cut away the rigging for the attack. Here we go!

In May 1718, Blackbeard anchored outside Charleston, plundered five ships, and stopped others from entering the port. He captured some leading citizens and threatened to execute them unless the town paid him off with medical supplies. For several days, Blackbeard heard nothing back. He was about to carry out his threat, when at last a message came through. The town agreed to his terms, and Blackbeard spared his captives.

Once the battle was won, we often set the crew of the prize ship free, if they were of no use to us. When Blackbeard took the *Concorde*, he forced the surgeons, carpenters, cooks, and pilot to join him.

# Booty Haul

Once we capture our prize ship, it's time to divide the spoils. Of course, Blackbeard takes the lion's share, but we pirates like to divide our booty. Gold and jewels are nice. But most ships don't carry them. What we usually get is food, cloth, tools, and weapons, which are far more useful to us. You can't eat gold when you're hungry! And you can't buy weapons out at sea. Sugar, wine, and tobacco are always nice treats after months living on stale beer and dry salty biscuits.

## Buried Treasure Myth

Robert Louis Stevenson's famous story *Treasure Island* gave people the idea that pirates often buried their stolen treasure, and then left maps with clues about where to find it. But only one pirate is known to have buried treasure—William Kidd. He hid his loot in 1701 when he thought he was going to be arrested. But he didn't leave a map. . .

## Pieces of Eight

A piece of eight was a Spanish silver coin. Pirates rarely saw them. But people often link them with pirates because in *Treasure Island*, Long John Silver's parrot keeps repeating "pieces of eight!"

# Pirate Haunts

After bagging that last prize, we can have a break! So we're off to Port Royal in Jamaica. Back in 1657, Port Royal let pirates come ashore in return for their protection from the Spanish. Soon every pirate on the oceans was sailing in to drink, gamble, and meet girls. It was so wild that people were soon calling it the most wicked city on Earth. Then, twenty-five years ago, Port Royal was overwhelmed by a devastating earthquake. It's just not the same now, they say. Still, I'm looking forward to getting my feet on dry land!

Even the local parrots and monkeys can be found at the inns in Port Royal! They say that's where Blackbeard found his pet monkey.

## Disaster Strikes

At 11:43 a.m. on June 7, 1692, an earthquake struck Port Royal. The city was utterly devastated, as buildings crumbled and sank into the sand. This disaster was followed by a tsunami that washed away half the city. Up to three thousand people died at once and two thousand more later, from disease. Most of the survivors moved to Kingston, which became the capital of Jamaica.

# Dressed Like a Pirate!

My own clothes wore out long ago. So I've got a new suit of pirate garb. We pirates have our own way of dressing. It's a mix of items stolen from our victims—and ones made from the rolls of luxurious cloth we rescued from a ship. Just like many of my fellows, my jacket's way too big for me, and my pantaloons are baggy and colorful. But I look every inch a pirate.

## Phrase Book

Pirates have their own way of talking...

**Shiver me timbers!** Expressing a nasty shock, based on the way the timbers (masts) shiver (shake) when hit by a cannonball

**Avast ye!** Stop (you)!

**Anchors aweigh!** Lift the anchor just clear of the bottom

**Landlubber!** The worst insult to a pirate. A lubber is someone clumsy, and who is happiest living ashore.

**Strike colors** Lower the flag and surrender

**Swabbie** A swab is a kind of mop, and a swabbie is the poor idiot who has to scrub all the blood off the decks after a fight. *Ugh!* That's me after I ran into the first mate by accident...

## Three-cornered Hat!

My proudest possession is my three-cornered or tricorne hat. Ordinary crew aren't allowed to wear them, but I'm Blackbeard's boy, now, so I've got one. Tricornes don't just look good. The broad brim keeps the ocean spray off your face, and the turn-up acts like a gutter.

# That's Your Lot

In November 1718, we were partying on Ocracoke Island off the Carolina coast when we saw two ships flying navy colors heading our way. With the tide out, they couldn't reach us over the sandbar that night. Next morning, as the tide rose and navy ships raced in over the bar, Blackbeard calmly steered his ship toward the beach. He must have gone mad! But then he steered us through a tiny gap between the beach and a sandbar. The navy ships slammed into the bar and stuck. *Aha!* But as our ship fired its cannon at them, it lurched back and soon we were stuck, too.

It looked like all the navy sailors had been killed by our cannon, so we rowed across and boarded their ship. Oh no, it was a trap. They were faking! The navy captain, Maynard, met Blackbeard face-to-face. They both fired pistols. But as Blackbeard swung his sword for the final blow, another sailor cut his throat from behind. That was the end of Blackbeard—and my life as a pirate! Hooray!

Many pirates who were caught alive were taken to London, tried, and then hanged—including Captain Kidd. The rope broke when they tried to hang Kidd, so they had to hang him a second time.

# Ten Peculiar Pirate Facts

**1** There were around two thousand pirates in the Caribbean in 1717.

**2** Pirates compensated men who were injured in battle. For example, a man who lost his right arm would receive six hundred pieces of eight or six slaves.

**3** If someone betrayed a pirate crew, they were sent an ace of spades playing card. This meant they were going to be killed. . .

**4** Some pirates really did have wooden legs. They often fought, and anyone badly wounded in the leg might need to have it cut off—to stop the gangrene (infection) from spreading and killing him.

**5** Pirates caught parrots in South America and taught them to talk. But they usually sold the parrots later for a high price.

**6** When Dutch pirate Dirk Chivers captured naval captain Sawbridge, the prisoner complained so much that Chivers sewed up his mouth with a needle and thread.

**7** In 1825, when pirates captured the ship *Eliza Ann*, they killed the crew. But they spared a woman— Lucretia Parker—who lived to tell the tale.

**8** Pirates liked to give their ships scary names. Benito de Soto called his the *Black Joke*. And Danish pirate John Derdrake's vessel had the ominous name *Sudden Death*.

**9** It was not uncommon for pirates to kidnap boys. Some boys, called "powder monkeys," had to keep the cannons topped up with gunpowder. Their life was very tough indeed!

**10** When Blackbeard was killed, his killers cut off Blackbeard's head and tossed his body over the side. It was said that his headless body still swam around, yelling, "Where's my head?"